SWEET SURRENDER

Reflections in Poetry and Prose

DOUG McPHILLIPS

Also, by Doug McPhillips:

Other Visionary Stories:
NOVELS.
From Darkness to Light.
Awake to my Gutted Dream.
The Sword of Discernment.
Santiago Traveller.
I Prophet.
Master's at my table.
The Guru of Jerusalem.
We are upside down. (Biography)
The Wicklow Way.
The Adventures of Ace McDice.
Instant Karma & Grace.
The Credo.
Reflections of an Old Man.
Reincarnation of the Assassin
Master of The Arts
Masters of Introspection.
King of the O' Malley
Journey to a hermit's haven.
The Rise and Rise of a 4th Reich
Grandad's tales are tall and true.
Into Action: Alcoholics for Jesus
Lightbulb Moments
For Pete's Sake
Walking in my Shadow
A Pilgrim's Last Hurrah
Camino Guide Book.
Country Camino. (Album).

Santiago Traveller. (Album).
Soul Fact. (Album).

Apart from any fair dealing for private study, research, criticism or review, as permitted under the Copyright Act, no part may be reproduced by any process without the editor's written permission.

Doug McPhillips Circa 2025 ISBN. 978- 1-7643804-8-5-9-2

National Library of Australia Catalogue-in-Publication data: New Holy Bible, International Version, Hodder & Stoughton, 1980. Alcoholics Anonymous, 4th Edition, AA World Service, 1976.
As Bill sees it, 8th Print, AA World Service. 2017
Daily Reflections, 11th Print, AA World Service 2014.
Journey to the Inner Mountain, Hodder & Staughton, James Cowan, 2002.
The Choice is always ours, Jove Publishing, 1997.
Santiago traveller, Ingram Spark, Doug McPhillips, 2018.
Chopping Wood, Short Run Press, David Bernz, 2023
Where have all the flowers gone? WW Norton & Co, 2006
The Times and Times of Bob Dylan: A Biography. Lulu Press,
Woody Guthrie- A Life- Joe Klein, Random House, 1999
Notebook Research.
Google research- Authors Unknown.

This book blends fact and fiction. All characters in this novel are either factual or fictional, and the names of people living at the time may be real or imagined. Any resemblance to actual events, locales, or persons, living or dead, is purely coincidental; however, what is applicable is indeed real. Where poetic license transforms fact into fiction, names have been altered to protect the innocent.

" Not I or anyone else can travel that road for you.
You must travel by yourself."

                    - Walt Whitman.

Content.

Introduction. 7.

Dawning light. 9.

Rainbows Gold. 11.

Twilight Horizons. 13.

The Crab Apple Tree. 15.

Walking in my Shadow. 17.

Track to Mission Mountain. 19.

Lessons in the living. 21.

Old Man at sidewalk cafe. 23

New Horizons. 25.

Mystery. 31

Silence. 35.

Detachment. 37.

Pilgrimage. 39.

Camino Wayward. 41.

Passing Moments. 45.

Nature, 49

The Dignity of Age. 51.

Consciousness. 55.

Sunday Morning. 59.

An Account of Stewardship. 65.

Overzealous. 67.

Multitasking. 69.

Myth 73.

Belonging. 75.

Divine Guidance 77.

Awareness. 79.

Beloved. 81.

Awakening. 83.

Surrender. 85.

Letting Go. 87.

Acceptance of Grace. 89.

God within the Silence. 93.

The Unhurried Soul. 97.

Divine Embrace. 99.

Flowing in Divine Love. 101.

The light of Grace. 103.

Closing Reflections. 105

Feeling the Letting Go. 107.

Introduction:

The story that begins here starts with a dream. The dramatist of the grace that follows was deeply asleep when a prophetic vision of a future event was sent to his subconscious. He was in a room with many people, some of whom were familiar to him and others with whom he was unfamiliar. Yet, they all waited eagerly for the author of these words, chosen by a chairperson sitting opposite them, to speak about the feeling of surrender.

The chairperson explained the gathering of like-minded individuals using overhead projector images, defining surrender as "a means to stop resisting and yield to the power or control of another, either by choice or under duress." The author was then asked to share his feelings about surrender. His mind immediately turned to analytical answers, such as letting go of something, stopping the attempt to control an emotion or situation, or relinquishing possession or control. He was lost in thought as the audience waited patiently for his response. Another phrase entered his mind, possibly embedded in his subconscious by his childhood religious upbringing, signifying a deep trust in God's love and His plan for us. Despite his efforts, he could not find the right words to express the feeling of surrender and was at a loss. For this dreamer, within the core of the message's purpose, he was called to relate but was not given to the emotion of "feeling surrender."

So it was then, upon awakening from the dream, that the author began this story, which he believes is best expressed in both poetry and prose. It recounts much of his life's journey of awakening towards the ultimate aim of "sweet surrender,' which is not just the title of this book but the purpose of humanity's journey, as he relates in the pages that follow.

In Genesis 1:27, it states that God created man in His own image, in the image of Himself, as male and female. The nature of the Godhead is challenging to define outside human understanding. Still, perhaps it can be said, for everyone's benefit, that God is an infinite intelligence beyond our capacity to comprehend fully. Therefore, through indoctrinated belief, symbols, signs, analytical studies, and imaginative reasoning, we gain some insight into that Godhead. A sensible person recognises a moral compass guiding righteousness and holiness, reflecting God's own statutes. In God, man has the capacity to be in harmony with nature as a thinking, reasoning being capable of exercising free will in reflection of God's intellect.

As humans, we recognise our ability to foster fellowship by reflecting God's own triune or singular nature and by loving one another in relationships. Being in God's image also includes having the authority to rule over the Earth and serve as God's representatives or ambassadors. Nonetheless, all humans are created in God's image; the fall into flawed behaviour has tarnished this image. However, it must be acknowledged that despite the damage, the image endures, evident in acts of civilisation, creation, love, and charity, though not perfectly reflecting God's original glory, if one adopts a religious perspective.

Suffice it to say that one can view this objectively from the humanist's perspective, or indeed from the atheist or agnostic perspective. In doing so, it cannot be denied that man has a choice to follow the dictates of his own conscience or fall into the nature of his defectiveness. Whatever your point of view, ultimately, surrendering is one's own unavoidable choice.

Dawning Light.

The darkness flickered into the first light within the mind's eye of man. A significant start of something new, the unfathomable enlightenment, of hope, of a new cycle offering another renewal and promise of creative vision through the mirror of possibility within matter, energy, space, and one day in the course of time. He had experienced that day for the past eighty years of his life. Awakening to a new beginning, through dawn, noon, and night. He was observing it now through the eyes and minds of memory, much like a chartist viewing a series of graphical images layered one on top of the other, to see the past tracking of his life, the present of his now, and to forecast with some insight into the future of where he is headed.

The observer might see an opposing side of this lifetime, noticing a pattern of wrong choices or reviewing good, orderly actions when they are aware of them. Alternatively, they might evaluate where and when opportunities in this life's journey were either unconsciously missed or deliberately ignored.

It was more about the present that he was now observing. With the benefit of hindsight, he understood his chosen paths more clearly than ever before, as he could now see moments of clarity — in creativity, in lessons learned through suffering inflicted upon him, or from those he caused — more often than not unconsciously. He now had the capacity to understand his charted history up to the present day and could fathom the direction choices he could make for his own wellbeing, as well as for the wellbeing of those he chose to serve. If he were then made in the image and likeness of God, then he had best behave as one.

Seeded Dawn.

Great blobs of fiery sunlight burst through the depths of dark, rippling across the leafy stillness as reality slowly sinks in on blinking eyes.

Streaming light dispels past blindness, and a new awakening gauges the skies' brightness.

The local sun rises, casting warmth on the delicate earth, while creations glisten with diamond-dew magic across the landscape.
The almighty beam of oceanic light tiptoes across the dawn as the last shadows of darkness fold back into the void.
Light penetrates the dreamtime, heralding a new beginning of natural love embrace in the beauty of the immeasurable sun.

With a spirit of universal clarity, the sunlight shapes the dawn, boldly resisting the causes of shadow, wind, and rain.
In the midst of this greater glory, in the arms of deep love, a new Adam embraces the beauty in a new-seeded dawn love!

Rainbow's Gold

He found himself challenged to confront the feeling of not truly being present. He had been in the sunlight of his day, yet drawn to darkness in the mind, as he drifted from the endless pursuit of ideas and actions, of one lover to another, of material pursuits that sifted through his fingers like the sands of time. He had been a driven soul for most of his life, and while he had the strength and capacity to achieve much in what he did, in the end, the purpose of his being seemed superficial. For all his experiences, youthful wisdom, and strength, it ultimately came to naught.

Time appears to be running out, and despite all his efforts to reach great heights, fear has made him realise that, no matter how brave he is or how much he desires it, chasing material things no longer excites him. He's getting older now, no longer possessing the strength and vitality he once had. He's travelled far on many adventures in search of freedom, unknowingly chasing what he would ultimately find in a new consciousness—his older, slower body and soul seeking experience through his feelings and surrender.

He was practising meditation and reflection just to be aware of the feelings bubbling inside him. He was in a state of stillness, feeling the cauldron of emotions he had formerly chosen to ignore, only to find them erupting uncontrollably from within. Now it was different; he could feel them deliberately without attaching himself to the emotional outcome. He regarded this spirit of stillness as his inner child, the place of his creative wealth, love, and understanding of his own godliness that he had finally begun to embrace instead of ignoring, as his lost former self once did.

Spirit Rainbow.

The sun's rays flash dark curtains open,
fiery eyes herald the sun,
Morning star on fading moon drops,
rain in mystic colours run,
directing dreamers to their goal,
somewhere beyond the rainbow's beam,

Stumbling dreamers, leading souls;
turning back from clouded night,
In your age of youth and wisdom,
You seek strength, both brave and bold.

When your body loses strength,
You are overcome by fear,
life's boldness no longer beckons,
For in truth, you're growing old.

Yet you seek the seed of wonder,
from beneath the rainbow's gold,
chains are breaking, freedom's dawning,
as you trudge the mountain's path.

Climb the highest peak to find,
stumbling down the vale below,
The pot of gold keeps on moving,
as a new rainbow unfolds.

Seek your God in desolate places,
That's what only we fools do,
Hark! Stay a while in spirit stillness,
the pot of gold's inside of you!

Twilight Horizon.

While recognising that feelings are not facts, without them, we are dead in the water—a drift in a sea of misery and discontent. Giving in to feelings is necessary, but only in a controlled manner. The path this person was on in pursuit of earthly glory brought the author of this story much grief and endless suffering for many a long day. He had to endure a lot to recover. The journey to this freedom of spirit has not been an easy one, and although he had dreamed many dreams that he transformed into creativity and adventure, he had not fully learnt to let go of his hold on worldly pursuits. He was in the process of doing so, for he would soon realise that he could not gain 'sweet surrender' to the spirit of his wholeness until he let go.

The world he had known for a long time, and despite achieving much fame and notoriety, couldn't fill or satisfy the void he longed to fill. He wasn't made to fit the ego-driven ideas he held. He was a square peg in a round hole, trying to find a place in a world of recognition, power, and prestige. He had worked hard to attain it, and the applause he relentlessly chased for decades ultimately proved to be an illusion.

He was still on a learning journey to overcome his flaws, walking his own path towards love. It made sense to him to entrust his life to God, and while his traditional beliefs hadn't entirely left him, he found that a Christ presence, without clear definition, was all he needed as a symbol to guide him, to entrust himself to, to be part of, to embrace without fear or favour. To let go as well, and to love. He had stopped praying regularly, yet in his mindful moments, that was all he longed for. He knew that a wholehearted love of God from him would make the shift from worldliness to godliness much easier, with a peaceful and prayerful handover to the God of his understanding.

Taken by the light.

There are paths I must follow,
ways of the spirit,
only God and little children
of the kingdom of heaven know.

Over time,
So much has been lost,
in sadness and shade,
We carry our cross.

Forgive and forget,
just keep moving forward,
Now is the time,
Just walk in your song.

Rise in God's divine light,
lead onward.
Keep our feet
on the path of love.

Christ in our presence,
release your fears,
walk in the springtime
of laughter and tears.

Pause in the flow of life,
step out there,
live in the moment,
Say a little prayer.

The Crab Apple Tree

In the middle of a friend's garden, a crab apple tree once stood. It was during the winter of my discontent that I felt a kinship with it, for it had, in that season, lost its leaves. Surrounding this tree was a collection of delicate evergreen and perennial plants that, despite the season, had, by nature, retained their leaves, awaiting once more the springtime of their buds and flowers.

The artistry of that friend, who has long since been lost to me, was like that of a horticulturist by trade, having forsaken her ability as a painter of still life to concentrate on creating a secret living garden of natural beauty in her own backyard. Her passion for growing those garden flowers would make even Adam in God's garden of Eden envious. For nothing she did, no matter how demanding, took away her joy in her passionate creation.

I know nothing about plant names, nor do I understand their Latin names. While I now recall the beauty I once saw in that backyard, I also remember that I somehow resonated more with the crab apple tree than with any other plant there. The crab apple, being a deciduous tree, had lost all its leaves. Like the hat tree, I have shed many layers of my outer shell and inner being recently due to significant events, both natural and unnatural, in my life. These events have sometimes left me raw and awkward as I slowly come to terms with life, with more and more of me becoming exposed to who I was and who I am becoming. For a time, it had the effect, particularly on cloudy, cold days, of drawing my mind into desolate places, in feelings of despair and hopelessness, and a sense of perhaps not ever rising above the loneliness and isolation of those feelings again.

It was then that I drew strength from the crab apple tree, even though it had seemed raw and awkward in its bare state, standing alone in a green garden. It somehow gave me the strength and courage to face life's challenges. As I look out my window now at a crab apple tree in my own flower garden, I notice the small buds and white flowers beginning to bloom in this early spring, having shed its previous appearance of cold, unloved emptiness. Like the crab apple tree of my past, I've shed the fragility of what once was to bloom and flourish in this mature phase of my life, to bloom through this spring.

In the twilight of my years, I watch patiently and cherish making the most of the remaining daylight before the sun dips below the horizon. From the darkness just before dawn, I await a new day with renewed patience and wonder, for there, as daylight streams through my window, my sight is greeted once more by the crab apple tree in the springtime of its life. My heart is therefore gladdened that my cycle of life continues to move through its seasons.

Walking in my shadow.

Do you see a flaming star? When you walk through clover fields, is God in your mind's eye or in your shadow? My mind is caught in a dream, walking this Camino path. You appear here as my shadow. So, you stay close by my side as I watch the pale moon rise. You appear here as my shadow. "So I sing out loud and clear, Love me, love me. Love me, dear, hold on now before I am invisible." Oh! You listen as I sing some unfamiliar theme. You appear here as my shadow. You are not here or there; you can't be touched with my hand. I cast my trouble to the wind and to my shadow. Now I call no place home, just walking here alone, heart set on my flaming star, you are my shadow. "So I sing out loud and clear, Love me, love me. Love me, dear, hold on now before I am invisible."

Just walking in a dream, arrows from the archers point the way, gold dust brushes my feet, followed by my shadow. This world has turned dark and grey, my shadows have abandoned me, and God's a stony path. Yes, he's my shadow. Yeah! I cry out to the moon, singing a joyful tune, casting fortune to the wind, and to my shadow. "So I sing out loud and clear, Love me, love me, Love me, dear, hold on now before I am invisible."

I have the choice to be rich or poor, to take pleasure as I wish, or simply walk this joyful road to my destiny. See my star shining brightly as I step into the night. The moon has now clouded over, and my shadow's disappeared. So, I carry my blazing star as I walk the Camino, singing, 'Love me, love me, love me, I am invisible.'

Soaking in tomorrow.

It's said that a road less travelled
may heal a broken heart,
blind faith in a God of light,
to guide you through the dark.

A friend in uncertain times,
where courage masks fear,
stepping into what may be,
wins over tears.

Gazing at a starry night,
soaking in tomorrow.

A life that's been broken needs
time to heal,
alone with nature's beauty,
bush birds and fresh, clean air.

Touched by sun-drenched rain and shadow.

Gazing at a starry night,
soaking in tomorrow.

Go gently, sleepy, broken heart,
let go of pain and sorrow,
to pass like fleeting friends,
for new horizons await.

Yes! All that was in yesterday,
will fade into the shadow,
Gazing at a starry night,
soaking in tomorrow!

There is a new life emerging,
 Your own will never be the same.
 New love, joy, and friendship
 will help you let go of pain.

Having gained wisdom through bitter sorrow,
You are on the path to freedom,
being stung by ageless wisdom,

Gazing at a starry night,
soaking in tomorrow.

Track to Mission Mountain.

There's a track to Mission Mountain,
It's the pathway of my dreams,
a way along the byway,
of valleys, hills, and streams.

An oath to a Godly purpose,
in the spirit plain above,
a reason for my living,
on a road to endless love.

There's a track in old Barque country,
where I found my way,
with a tent, knapsack, and a tucker bag,
I waltzed the Matilda way.

Walking the Spanish highlands,
on the Camino,
walking the Spanish highlands,
on the Camino.

So sweet muse of Mission Mountain,
the source of light and love,
lead on, this weary traveller,
to tramp the path to love.

There is nature's endless wonder,
by valleys, hills, and streams,
bringing all now to reality,
not just in my dreams.

There's a track in old Barque country,
where I found my way,
with a tent, a knapsack, and a tucker bag,
I waltzed the Matilda way.

Walking the Spanish highlands,
on the Camino,
walking the Spanish highlands,
on the Camino.

Lessons in the living.

When we have longed to reach a goal for many years and finally achieve it after numerous struggles and hardships, we expect to feel content, fulfilled, and at peace. Yet all too often, the opposite occurs. We can't understand why, having climbed to the top of the mountain, the sense of achievement and contentment somehow slips away from us. When we return to the valley floor, the view can seem both impressive and bleak, even hopeless. Whether it's a position of worldly responsibility or the pursuit of material things, many of us are driven— or so it appears—by the need to have something, to win something, to gain something, or to be someone other than ourselves. Yet our journey reveals a secret of the human heart: it is not the prize but the struggle that makes us feel alive, to which we give our greatest love and commitment. And although we are reluctant to admit it, it is the struggle that brings out the best in us.

Throughout most of my life, I have followed a pattern of striving for success, seeking recognition, and chasing material wealth. I reached my lowest point when everything I had worked for collapsed, and I fell into confusion, health problems, and despair—depressed to the very core of my being in the darkness of my soul. Like an old knight, I took up a symbolic lotus of creative ideas and began to write stories with courage, hope, and a desire to succeed, despite my personal hardships.

Now, after years of adventures and countless stories, inspired ideas in the pursuit of creating for the greater good, what does one do with this powerful, impetuous, noble spirit when the cause for fighting on is no longer alive? The fruit has withered on the vine, some of the branches are now dead, but do I keep hanging around with words of discernment, doing my best to water the remaining vines in the hope they might still bear fruit?

Should I be there to rejuvenate my offspring, or those of my friends and the wider community, despite my lack of enthusiasm for the task? Yes, I must take responsibility and use my God-given talents to do so. While life teaches us that we humans need first to pursue our personal ambitions, we still belong to a larger community. We should contribute to the greater good so life can flow within us once more.

Over time, we start to reflect on what the struggle has truly been for and whom or what it ultimately serves. Therefore, we might consider planting another mustard seed to nurture a different great work, this time for one's spiritual well-being rather than focusing on the benefits to humanity, which, upon full reflection, could still be another ego-driven notion. If we turn to our Higher Power, whether that be within as something intangible or in nature, then that is where we may grow.

In this moment of reality, we become more determined to let go of youthful things and, through sometimes misguided pathways, step into the great unknown with newfound wisdom and confidence, shedding the insecurities of youth and focusing more on appreciating life itself and building genuine relationships. The focus slowly shifts from superficial appearances to inner beauty, which opens the door to stories that have always existed and are now evolving from the inner child to be shared anew.

Old man at the sidewalk cafe.

There's an old man at the sidewalk cafe,
drinking his coffee slowly,
just sitting there taking it easy;
no longer on the go.

Is that the old man who made a fortune?
The hero of Big Dome and Co?
Did he see it crumble?
Or did he just let it go?

He's the old man at the sidewalk cafe,
who lived like some Peter Pan,
believing there was a better way
In some Never Never land!

Oh! He knows his time is fading,
The sunsets are kicking in,
He can hear the bell tolling,
Is it ringing just for him?

See the old man at the sidewalk cafe,
drinking his coffee neat,
lost in a dream of past glory,
fading so slowly with him.

He knows his days are numbered,
like every man that lives,
seeing the cards he has been dealt,
living and dying with him.

See the old man at the sidewalk cafe,
doing the best that he can,
learning to live, love and let go,
Starting all over again?

See the old man at the sidewalk cafe,
watching the passing parade,
just sitting there taking it easy,
no longer on the go.

Maybe it's not too late,
The game of patience, the go,
waiting for the hand of fate
just sitting there taking it easy…

With the hope of one last deal?

New Horizons.

Historically, this author has explored many new horizons on his life's journey toward inner joy, peace, and understanding. He has concluded that there is no secret to life except to accept whatever comes. Deep inside, he longed for the peace of knowing the Higher Spirit that created him—a uniquely soulful being with a strong ambition to reach new heights of awareness. It was in examining who he is that he turned to his feelings, which became the heart of the matter and the focus that led to writing this book. Many times in the past, he looked inward to observe his feelings and expectations. It always seemed that during times of difficulty, suffering, or emotional or physical illness, he found the time to sit quietly and observe himself meditatively. Now it had come to this again, as he struggled to write lines about his feelings, for without contemplating them, he had no hope of surrender. The result of his emotional responses had sparked his creativity, for he had previously fallen into the dragon's mouth, driven by fear and dread, only to emerge with a lotus of innovative ideas.

He endured the agony of uncontrollable calamity, which unintentionally led to a physical and mental collapse. Only then, like many others he had read about or seen firsthand, he cried out for help. It was then that he learned to trust in the slow work of God. As he peeled back the lotus flower, he recovered and produced works in books and songs that he believed were aimed at others. Now, it was different, for he had reached a part of himself that required the discipline to remain still.
Starting a new adventure was always the plan, but this time it felt different. The author now realised he needed to sit with his feelings for a while before putting pen to paper to share his thoughts fur-

ther. He must feel and accept those visual images first, before he can truly let go. Otherwise, how would he ever understand the sweet surrender he was after, without ego notions of the shadow self, relying only on a logical, linear explanation?

Yet, a logical, linear evaluation is necessary for many daily life events; otherwise, there would be no progress, nothing to assess or value, no way to measure advancement or retreat, and everything would be lost in a void. So, in one's old age, having endured the ups and downs of fortune, what is wrong with living in a void?

In Japanese kanji, there is a symbol called "mu," which essentially signifies "nothing" or "no-thing." It isn't used in everyday conversation, but it serves a purpose here as it relates to the void, where it can be interpreted as the space where one is mindful of one's own understanding of God. It is here that we may have a silent dialogue with the power that makes us who we are. Here, we learn to let go of worldly desires, of all that baggage that holds us back from a sweet surrender to this infinite intelligence. For this author, there is no need to face feelings of abandonment, the pain of loss, or suffering, much less the need to express joy, happiness, or contentment. It is a state of acceptance, of living in the present and being aware of the moment, whether that emptiness transforms into deep surrender. In this state, a sense of utopian living prevails — an ideal of living in a world that does not truly exist.

The author must then understand reality if he is to live at all. When examining reality, it is seen as the totality of everything that truly exists, independent of thoughts or perceptions, including both physical and potentially non-physical aspects of the world. It is distinct from imaginary, conceptual, or theological ideas and is the fascinating subject of fields such as metaphysics, which explore the nature of existence. It exists and has its own nature, whether he is willing to recognise it or not. It does not depend on his perception to continue existing. He understands that the senses and the human mind are the primary ways we interact with reality. Reality extends beyond the material world, encompassing non-physical realms such as mental states, universal forms, or abstract ideas. Whatever it means to him, or indeed to you, the reader, it simply is.

Thus, in his later years, the author learns to live again in a realm of acceptance, embracing what it means to be, letting go in the present, and living with whatever arises in the mind, heart, or soul. For what has passed, he cannot change, except to learn the lesson that it has presented to him, for better or worse. When it comes to the future, he cannot predict it with certainty, but he can draw on the wisdom of having lived, learnt, and applied it to the present moment. He must navigate it moment by moment, accepting what is, and, in doing so, master himself enough to let go in a gentle surrender at any given time.

Utopia.

Walking on this mystic path,
 seeing the sun set in a violet sky,
 passing signposts along the way,
 a gateway to my destiny,
 Good karma is on high.

Reflecting on dreams to come,
learning from the past,
feeling the presence on the way,
listening to inner sounds,
destiny on firm ground.

It's the oneness of being,
in the newness of time,
letting go of emotional baggage,
heading to Utopia,
heading to Utopia,

Oh! You know the way of the spirit,
 time and energy in your stride,
 keep the spirit of your mindset,
 and faithful pilgrims by your side,
 living in the moment of Utopia.

The lesson of the Camino.
 to clear old karma,
 reset the soul's direction,
 on a track less travelled by,
 a way to reincarnation,

Heading for Utopia.
There is light upon the pathway,
good karma in your stride,
meditating in the moment,
Mindfulness is the way,
heading for my shelter,
Heading for Utopia.

The planets are aligned,
The days are warm and sunny,
night skies are diamond starlight,
There is magic in your eyes,
When you get The Way,
Heading for Utopia.

Oh! You understand the way of the spirit,
energy and time in your stride,
keep the spirit of your mindset,
and faithful pilgrims by your side,
living in the moment of Utopia.

" I said to my soul, be still, and wait without hope
　For hope would be for the wrong thing;
　wait without love
　For love would be love of the wrong thing;

There is yet faith
　But the faith and the love and the hope
　They are all in the waiting.
　Wait without thought, for you are
　not ready for thought:
So the darkness shall be the light
And the stillness of the dancing."

T.S. Eliot, 'East Coker, Four Quartets.

Mystery.

A mystery unfolds when we let life happen naturally instead of pushing it. It's that strange knock on the door, a quick glimpse of a flower blooming without fuss, an arvo in the backyard, or a day riding the midtown bus. To see. To notice. Just to be there.

There is something sacred in simply believing that what happens to us each day is meant to awaken our souls to something new: a different smell, a new taste, a moment when we make eye contact with a stranger, smile a little, or nod in greeting. Who knows? Perhaps one of those things will reconnect us to the refreshing memory of pain, a meaningful reminder of glory, a gasp of astonishment, or a sense of God's presence in life.

The sunlight reveals new shades of colour, rekindling the significance of a long-past moment. Astonishment jolts us into a conscious awareness of things that have been seen but also long hidden. These things are central to mystery.

There is a purpose to mystery in a cool, calculated world. We live lives that are now so precisely timed. Before people owned watches, dawn and dusk provided enough of a framework to live by. "I'll come tomorrow" meant I would be there when I arrived the next day. Now, "I'll come tomorrow" only specifies the time down to the minute, exactly to the moment. No mystery there. Just expectation.

So, mystery—the idea that something incredible can happen at any moment if we make space for it—leads us to a new awareness of God's presence in time. God comes, we understand now, when we least expect it. Perhaps most of all, when we least expect it.

With age, mystery becomes more vivid. Nothing feels certain anymore. Everything hints at the possibility of anything. I might still be here. And I might not. Like children, we learn to wonder again. We understand that getting up each day can be a challenge, but it can also be a beautiful experience. Something will definitely happen. What will it be?

Then, as the years pass, we learn to trust the goodness of time, the glorious bounty of life that is God. And who knows? At the end of life, the mystery that awaits us finally becomes clear.

Love.

Is it the sound I'm hearing in the trees?
Do I see you in the falling leaves?
Maybe it's the sweetness of the breeze,
the feel of sand between my toes.

We did our mating in some distant past,
Life was always splendid in the grass,
Now feelings are faded memories,
And nothing ever lasts for long.

Is it the woman cradled in my arms,
the warmth of her constant charms,
maybe it's the child upon my lap,
that sense of innocence.

Oh! Love,
Come back into my room,
and take away these blues.

Did I see you in the corner of my eye?
The shadow of the bird flying by,
the warmth of the sun upon my face,
maybe now in a fading cloud.

Did I see you somewhere on the road?
Was it a gentle hand upon my back,
maybe it's the burden of the load,
When I look back.

We came together, staring into space,
listening to the sound between the chords,
dancing our way together in the rain,
There, we just died in tune.

Oh! love,
Come back into my room,
and take away these blues.

Now I'm here out upon the track,
walking with a knapsack on my back,
taking the rough with the smooth,
Looking for the love that I once knew.

Are you there with the man in the moon,
Did I see you in a shooting star?
The flash of light in a star-studded sky,
that faded out too soon.
Is it true you were here at the start?
Maybe back there in my mother's womb,
Where are you now, my gentle one?
Is it because I am lost and worn?

Now I am here out upon the track,
walking with my knapsack on my back,
taking the rough with the smooth,
Looking for the love that I once knew.

Oh! love,
Come back into my room,
and take away these blues.

Yesterday we did cartwheels on high,
laughed a lot until we said goodbye,
and the wheel is still in spin,
hoping you'll return again

We came together, staring into space,
listened to the sound between the chords,
danced our way together in the rain,
Then we just died in tune.

Now I'm here out upon the track,
walking with my knapsack on my back,
taking the rough with the smooth,
Looking for the love that I once knew.

Silence.

And Moses said to Aaron: this is what God was referring to when he said 'with those close to me I will be sanctified, and before the entire nation I will be honoured', and Aaron was silent…(Lev 10:3)

"There is a time to be silent and a time to speak" (Kohelet 3:7).

There is a silence that is "a very eloquent silence, a screaming silence, a shouting silence." If someone has a lot to say but chooses not to, "that suggests the power of silence." (Elie Wiesel's powerful perspective on silence:) The silence within can be both protective and painful. The unthinkable silence—the unspeakable, the ineffable, the inarticulable, the unnoticed, the unknowable, and the unconceptual. Whatever our circumstances, we must come to terms with them, and it is in that silence that they resonate, despite the pain and suffering we must endure. Ultimately, we need to confront our inner demons, for we cannot escape them. **There exists an inner cauldron of bubbling emotions that has been simmering since the moment we take our first breath. It is the feeling that our shadow self feeds on, urging us towards the seven deadly distractions of pride, covetousness, lust, anger, gluttony, envy, and sloth—the pleasurable diversions that steer us away from the pain of suffering, from endurance in the silence of our souls.**

It is in nature that the sounds of silence resonate most deeply with the spirit within. The gentle sounds of a breeze rustling through the leaves, cicada calls, a bird in flight, the buzzing of bees, and a babbling creek all form a harmonious chord that speaks to our hearts, no matter life's challenges. These moments of grace bring us into harmony with the soul.

Then there is the juxtaposition of a demand for silence. Those with a disgruntled spirit, disturbed by nature.

I wished a bird would fly away,
and not sing by my house today.

The fault must have been partly mine,
The bird was not to blame for its key.

And of course, there must be something wrong
In wanting to silence any song.

- Robert Frost.

Detachment.

It has taken this author a lifetime to start learning the art of detachment—the act of disengaging or separating something, and the state of being disengaged or separated; disconnection.

While healthy detachment has shown me that setting boundaries can safeguard mental well-being, unhealthy detachment can prevent forming relationships, sharing feelings. It may point to deeper issues like trauma or mental health concerns. My time in rehab for depression and anxiety involved struggling to let go of past problems. It required significant healing, venturing into the unknown, meditation, and exploring my stories before I understood detachment. Although emotional detachment can be a healthy way to manage emotions, it can become harmful when overused and damage your mental health.

I'm still learning to create space for myself so I can think clearly and stay separate, while remaining kind and loving. Here's the bottom line: You can feel compassion for someone else without needing to act on it. You can support another person without having to take any action or say anything. Detaching now means stepping back from obsessively worrying about others, telling them what to do, and trying to rescue them from their choices. To overcome emotional detachment, it's important to build self-awareness through mindfulness, journaling, and practices related to the body and emotions. I sought professional help to understand the roots of detachment and learn coping skills. I nurtured a supportive social network, practised vulnerability with trusted individuals, and engaged in self-care and creative outlets to reconnect with my inner self and express emotions safely.

Wayfarer.

Once, I was a wayfarer,
Caught the sun in flight,
Wild woman, drink and laughter,
Danced my day and night.

All just faded to nothing,
Waste of life, so it seems,
Like casting a stone into water,
watching the wake subside.

So I turned to work for Wander,
Chasing the money and power,
Had my fame and fortune,
It lasted for an hour.

'Twas then I married a lover,
Raised me a family,
but she left for another,
Tasted the fruit of the lemon tree.

It all just faded to nothing,
Waste of life, so it seemed
Like casting a stone into water,
Watching the wake subside.

Well, I took my share of lovers,
I watched my kids grow up,
Carried a torch for adventure
Drank my share of the cup.

Oh! It all just faded to nothing,
Waste of life, so it seemed,
Like casting a stone into water,
Watching the wake subside.

Pilgrimage.

Adventurer, my first step into the world came after much hardship and sadness. I was still letting go of many attachments to my past pains and the grief over the big losses I had faced over the previous decade. The journey didn't seem to me as one might have imagined at the time. It arrived by chance, through a medallion symbol I found on a city street a year before I felt drawn to walk the Camino de Santiago. I had picked it up from the footpath. The medallion featured a stick-figure image on its front, walking along a mountain trail with arms outstretched, holding walking poles, as if expressing a sense of freedom. Flying away from the man's head was a black raven, and the sun shone brightly in the sky. Around the border of the image was a river with turbulent, flowing water, yet with a calm aspect in the deeper parts. At the bottom of the medallion was a symbol, a Christian cross. I turned the medal over to see an image of a pilgrim's staff. I was feeling down then, in a deep cloud of despair, and that small prophetic medallion held little meaning for me at the time, but I attached it to my car keyring and didn't think much more about it until I started my first camino with it.

Upon re-examining the medallion, I noticed another distinct feature: a triangular shape at the base of the pilgrim stick figure's feet. In hindsight, it was prophetic that I walked the Camino de Santiago across the Pyrenees for the first time. The depression I left on the route resembled the raven's departure on the medallion. I had two walking poles then and had been attending Alcoholics Anonymous for some time before my pilgrimage. The AA symbol is a triangle with three words on its sides: Unity, Service, and Recovery. The reverse side of the medallion on the walker's staff, which I used before I bought walking poles, holds significance. The crucifix at the base of the medallion resonates with me, too, as it has a spiritual connection to a higher power, serving as a guide and protector in my recovery from illness and in my return to health and sobriety.

We are given signs to guide us on our life's journey, which we often overlook because we are not fully present in the moment. These messages for our best direction come in the form of symbols and signs, such as artefacts, nature, and interactions with other people. It was this author's experience to walk three pilgrimages on the Camino de Santiago over the next decade, write many books and songs as a means of coming to terms with his best direction in life, and to use his creative talents for the benefit of other travellers on life's journey.

From my experience, pilgrimage doesn't have to be about covering a specific distance, nor does it need a famous destination, sacred or not. It does, however, require an intention, and I believe this is the key to the healing power of pilgrimage. It also sets it apart from simply 'going for a walk'. For healing to occur during pilgrimage, I've found that we must immerse ourselves in the landscape and somehow bring the landscape into us, creating a reconnection to our environment that I believe is dangerously lacking in human awareness today.

Could many physical and mental illnesses arise from this disconnection, from viewing ourselves as separate from the very world we live in? In our culture and society, we often see ourselves as entities that exist on Earth rather than within or of it.

Camino Wayward.

It has been eight years since I walked 'The Way' of my third Camino. I have travelled the sacred path that pilgrims have followed for over a thousand years, from the medieval days of the Templar Knights to the present day. The Way is a journey of awakening and enlightenment. It taught me not to be burdened by need, or even the desire, for material possessions that society often equates with success.

My first Camino pilgrimage was a way to shed my inner faults. Because I valued life experiences so much, I believed that my own foolishness ultimately led nowhere, which pushed me into depression, anxiety, and alcoholism. The journey on that Camino opened up a lotus flower of creative ideas within me, resulting in books and songs that I have since written and sold. They became my salvation—doing something meaningful for myself and others, a path I continue to follow today. Then came the second Camino, through Portugal, which led me to leave one lover and seek another, who, for a time, proved to be my undoing. From that, I learnt through heartache the true wisdom of love over lust. Finally, I returned to the Camino Frances, my third pilgrimage, to walk The Way once more — the journey I took for my own inner wellbeing. And although I trekked nearly 1,200 kilometres through rain, hail, and shine, I have little to show for it, except for more creative ideas and a couple of albums of songs.

There is, however, the realisation that 'The Way' involves some movement towards inner discovery and personal growth. We learn to meet and overcome resistance, fears, grief, grievances, and old emotions we have struggled with before. Just as we put down our backpacks to rest along the way, we learn to set down our emotional baggage, too. Then we grow and find it easier to tune into a broader and more profound consciousness of the beauty around us, the 'peace within,' the interconnectedness of everything and everyone, a benevolent force that seems to guide us, and so on. At least that is what this author retells himself, but the process is not finished with letting go and peeling back the lotus flower; it continues trudging towards the ultimate good of all involved and working for the benefit.

Creations of the Heart.

In the mind's eye of a dreamer
It's a quest,
like an artist carving images
from stone,
Maybe there is nothing on
the other side,
Just some crumbling stone.

Still, the living can take shape.
In the mind of man,
Ideas always have new forms
In a heart of stone,
Walking on this pathway,
On my way home.

In the mind's eye of the dreamer,
Life has meaning,
joins the artist, carving forms
New life takes shape,
springs the twinkling of the stars,
In the dream, there is reason,

for the stone's new shape.
Perhaps that's why the cowboy
rides the ranges,
burning eyes of coal
in the night's log fire,
walking on some lofty hill
at midnight,
seeking out the home
of his desire.

How shall we view
The Temple of Creation,
sense the obstacles dissolve,
In some sacrifice,
for the working of the mind
a crucifixion,
on the dressed altar,
the mind's creative light.

Many are the instruments
of the searching,
The workings of the mind,
the body, soul,
seeking out some magic
of the utterance,
in coloured painted clay,
in human stone.

Hear the strings pluck
at the chords,
sound vibrations,
In the brass or reed,
cries the voice,
in a hammered tone,
primary dance of the body,
a movement of the human soul's state.

Perhaps it's why the cowboy
rides the ranges,
burning eyes of coal
in the night's log fire,
walking on some lofty hill
at midnight,
seeking out the home
of his desire.

Passing moments.

When we consider the shadow lands of our lived life—whether it has been a life fully experienced, by chance, through risky liaisons, as an adventurer, or in the endless fatigue of having been there and done that—most of us recall moments through thoughts, words, and deeds filled with happiness, pain, and sadness, as well as moments of great achievement, only to see them ultimately crumble and fade into nothingness. At least, this has never been my experience in the seen world, but what about the invisible, eternal things?

A day will come when I will put away the backpack forever, stop writing many books, and watch them all fade into dust. The only memory will be when some thoughtful soul searches for me and finds a brief, fading comment from artificial intelligence about the legacy — or lack of it — I have left for humanity. That will be all of me that remains, as it is for any man. Perish the thought, as we all wish to live longer, but to what end if life is merely an endless pursuit of ideas and actions that ultimately amount to nothing? When all we have built collapses, and the material, the prompt, and the ceremony fade into the mists of time, what can we honestly say it has been for?

It has been written in the spiritual texts of old that there is a house built by God for us, and we shall receive our just reward when we leave this mortal coil and enter the eternal kingdom. It follows that we are to live for God as much as our duty to our fellow man, while we live and breathe here. Still, in our aging, decaying bodies, we find it difficult to let go of earthly pleasures—rewards that are here today and gone tomorrow. Wiser heads than mine have written that the temporal life is the seed of eternal life. The things a man sows, so shall he reap in eternity. Therefore, what is it that requires our stewardship for the remainder of our lives? Should we live today to die tomorrow?

Overall, when considering the checks and balances of life, regardless of its ups and downs, I have realised that the symbols and signs in our daily lives are present in every dull and joyful moment—if I am truly aware enough to notice them from an eternal perspective rather than just through the feelings I experience. It is my duty, now more than ever, to surrender to a power greater than myself for guidance and action in truly living—living as if there is no tomorrow. Perhaps it's because I have been a tough nut to crack that the God of my understanding has granted me a length of days? Still, mine is not to question why; mine is but to do or die. In recent days, I've learnt that life is not all about me.

Growing In Grace

Is it gracious that I am
In growing old
Accepting the body's age
In weakness and infirmity?

The youth vanished so fast.
In the twinkling of an eye
Strength I took for granted
And enthusiasm faded.

In my middle age,
I came to know
The getting of wisdom
Many times I failed you.

You entrusted me

With children
And for others to follow
And even more, I let you down.

Perhaps that's why
I'm still around
As an old guide
Off the light to shine?

I laboured diligently
For as long as I could
Now it's time to do less
But pray to make good.

The fabric I am wearing
Is worn as I am
As twilight sets in
And worries are fading.

For I dance in the shadows
And laugh at the night
Embracing the silence
in the fading of light.

So in the arms of the dusk
I sing my sweet song
To each line of soft note
Where I now belong.

For growing old gracefully
It's not about years
But to live in the moment
Of laughter and tears.
So here's to the journey

Of what's been, yet to come
Of the courage found deep
In reliable friends..

With a full heart
Full of love, as it seems
Free spirit set free
Like a flower in bloom

Ashes to ashes
And dust to dust,
That time will come
In parting, we must.

Oh! Let not Death's shadow,
Come sooner than I wish
There is much to be done
And living is bliss.

I should not wonder
It's in the Universal plan
For man to mirror God
As God mirrors man.

Nature.

In our modern world, we often overlook the natural surroundings of the bush, sea, and sky. Immersing oneself in natural environments — plants, animals, and landscapes — offers substantial physical and mental health benefits, such as reducing stress, lifting mood, and increasing physical activity. It involves building a deep, connected relationship with the environment, fostering a sense of belonging, and embracing a simpler, slower pace of life that contrasts with the fast-paced urban lifestyle. This way of living can include sustainable practices, self-sufficiency, and an appreciation for the interconnected rhythms of the natural world.

A wanderer in the bush, far from everything and without company, has always brought me healing. In the depths of a forest, we forget our connection to the world. There's no one around to talk about trees, fish in a flowing stream, birds, or bees. Words aren't needed to express what something is. There, you don't need a word to describe the buzz of bees. What exists in nature in that environment has its own wordless language. It's simply part of the daily experience of living with what unfolds in the shadowy forests. You feel it, see it, hear it, breathe it, and be aware of it. Through observation, you learn to tune in with it and understand nature's language. So, in the mystery of it all, it is what enables a spiritual being, like a human, to have a human experience.

The phrase "you can't see the forest for the trees" indicates that someone who is unaware might focus too much on small, individual details or problems, missing the bigger picture or overall situation. Being overwhelmed by specifics and losing sight of the broader context can often be the cause. Taking a walk in the bush now and then helps reconnect us with nature, grounding us and renewing our ability to handle life's complexities while staying in tune with nature's spiritual connection.

Soul Shattered Miracle.

We are but shattered pieces
of a mirror in the void,
A universal reflection
as the light into darkness comes.

A mirror of a prism
beaming visions of illumination,
a dull reflection of the glory
In thought, word, and deed.

Man cannot recreate
The mirror of creation,
But can conceive
Some order out of chaos.

This godly world is a miracle,
A dream beyond belief
In unity of purpose
All things are possible.

In a one world united,
where love rains, hate is dead
The world's wounds can be mended,
Let the miracle begin.
This Godly world is a miracle,
As oneness we are God,
In unity of purpose,
All things are possible.

The Dignity of Age.

The garden was silent, as if time itself had held its breath. Beneath a cypress tree that had witnessed centuries pass, two figures met — one dressed in the white robes of Rome, the other in the relaxed attire of the modern day. Between them, no clock ticked, no shadow shifted. Philosophy alone marked the hour.

In this modern moment, a man reflects on the past and asks a wise philosopher: "Marcus Tulles Cicero — two thousand years, and your words still reach us. I have come seeking your wisdom, for our age fears old age as if it were a sickness, rather than a natural part of life." Then, as if by magic, the philosopher responds: For it is Cicero: Ah, my friend, men feared age even in my time. Yet the years, if rightly borne, are the richest part of life. I once wrote that *"Old age is the crown of life, our final act of reason."* Tell me, does your age not see it so?" The modern man, considering his own age and the life he led, views this as a question about the seasons of his life and those of others, and what has transpired over time: "We measure worth by youth — by the speed of our limbs and the freshness of our faces. The elderly are often overlooked, their counsel unheeded. The world runs fast and leaves them behind." He is mindful of his own twilight years and now clearly hears the words of the great philosopher, to which he is destined to take heed.

Cicero, with finger to his chin and a faint smile on his lips, replies: Then you're world runs without reflection. Youth is fire — it lights the way, yes — but it burns quickly. Age is the hearth: steady, enduring, giving warmth long after the flame has fallen. Wisdom, like wine, ripens in stillness.

Even though the modern man is of senior years, he still has a spring in his step, passion in his desire, and an unanswered feeling in his heart: "But tell me, Cicero, what of decline? The mind slows, the body falters. How can a man find dignity in the fading of strength?" Cicero, with ponderous thought, gives breath and space with his response, for he does not wish to offend the modern man who is still searching despite his dotage. "He must not mistake movement for worth. A tree bears fruit in its season, and in winter, it gives shelter. The old man's vigour lies not in his limbs but in his counsel, in the tempered calm that no storm can shake."

The modern man, who is aware of the needs of his era, responds: "In our time, we speak of 'retirement' — as if a man must step back from usefulness once his career is finished." Cicero is somewhat taken aback by this way of thinking and firmly replies: "A foolish invention! The soul does not retire. The statesman, the thinker, the teacher — all continue their work even when the crowd no longer cheers. To converse with one's own mind, to study, to reflect — these are the labours of the later years, and they are noble ones."

The modern man defends himself, almost challenging Cicero, by saying: "You speak of reflection, but many in old age feel isolation. Companions fade, families scatter, and silence grows long." Cicero, a man of great depth of character, with knowledge and wisdom from his era in the political arena of the Roman Senate, does not grow impatient but responds with great authority: "Yes, I too knew solitude — in exile, in disfavour, even in Rome's Senate where friends were few and envy loud. Yet solitude can be a friend if one has learned to converse with wisdom. Books, memory, and virtue — these never desert a man."

So at this point, the modern man prefers the belief of the wise one: then the faithful companion of age is not another person, but one's own cultivated mind.

"Precisely," cries Cicero. "The unexamined life leaves the old man empty. But he who has lived with thought finds that age gives him a deeper 'peace'— the calm after the tempest of ambition. The mind, seasoned by experience, becomes its own philosopher."

Then exclaims the modern man, for he is still afraid of the end of his time as if he were not fulfilled: "And what of death, Cicero? For many, it is the shadow that makes old age bitter.

Cicero: "Ah, death — the final argument. I once feared it, as do all men. But over time, I saw that it is not the enemy of life, but its completion. He who has lived well should not dread the end, for his work is woven into the fabric of those who follow."

Modern man: "That is the dignity of age, then — not merely to endure, but to transmit, to leave something of the spirit behind."

So it was that Cicero did the summary up of his belief:

Indeed. The dignity of age lies in its offering — the harvest of thought, the tempering of passion, the stillness that instructs the young. When a man carries his years with grace, he becomes a bridge between worlds — the living memory of what endures.

The breeze softly ruffled the leaves, and when the modern lad turned to reply, Cicero was gone. Yet his words remained — not as an echo, but as understanding.

And so, across two thousand years, wisdom once again found a listener.

A Poem of Age.

The years arrive like gentle rain,
Not stealing youth, but softening pain.
The mirror's truth, though lined and clear,
Reflects not loss — but what was dear.

For time, that sculptor, slow and wise,
Carves depth behind the steady eyes;
And in the hush of autumn's breath,
There hums no fear, no talk of death.

The heart, though slower, beats more truly.
It loves not many, but the few
Whose souls have walked beside its flame,
and need no youth to feel the same.

The hands that once rushed to build and fight,
the words that once roared
 now softly teach,
 of things no rush or gold can attain.

So let the young chase fleeting days,
and lose themselves in life's bright maze;
for we who stand where shadows blend,
know dusk is not the dark — but end.

For age is not the loss of grace,
but time's long kiss upon the face;
 a gentle crown, both stern and kind,
the final flowering of the mind.

Consciousness.

It's only after truly living life—reaching an age when wisdom finally settles upon us—that we come to understand how the darkness that once overshadowed our dreams becomes our most excellent enlightened teacher. While we may have been suitable for a time, our faults inevitably come to light. In truth, we become even more aware of our flaws when we strive to improve but fall short more often than we think is fair.

We remember the wild days of restless youth, when our attitude was, *"Eat, drink, and be merry, for tomorrow we die."* It was fear that drove us on—fear, or the fleeting thrill of glory in winning—yet ultimately it was the pain of regret that caught up with us. Nearing death, we start to see through the illusions of it all. We may be weary or blind, but behind the mask we catch a glimpse of quiet joy. We curse the fire that no longer pushes us toward our former glory.

And in that moment of living fully in the Now, we become aware that we have *lived a dream* — we have dreamed, we are dreamt — and at last, we may live consciously, awaiting the enlightenment of the One who created us, whose gentle guidance leads us towards the eternal.

What do we mean by consciousness? Is it simply being fully aware? Our life has brought us to this: the arrow from Cupid's bow has finally pierced our hearts, and with whatever remains of life, we must surrender—regardless of the feelings of the moment or the unanswered fears that linger with us. Our minds stop futilely dwelling on images, yesterday's regret, tomorrow's hopes. No, it is living in the moment, not overthinking anything except what is happening for us right now. In that, through our life experiences, we are fully conscious and await the next best thing that is present to us as our maker guides us to be.

Picture someone waking at dawn. At first, there's only a faint glow of light, the gentle rhythm of breath, and the quiet beat of a heart. Then awareness begins to grow. The person notices the warmth of the sun, the weight of the body, and the thoughts forming like ripples across a still lake. In that moment of seeing, something incredible is happening — consciousness is stirring.

At its simplest, consciousness is the gentle realisation: *"I am here. I exist."* It is the inner light through which we experience life. It enables us to taste joy, feel sorrow, learn, grow, question, and wonder. It is the silent witness behind every thought, the observer watching the mind, the awareness that knows it is aware.

So, I have travelled the road of life mostly unaware, but in these later years I have finally evolved from my previous state of being. I am now conscious.

As life unfolds, consciousness deepens. We begin to see not only the world around us but also the world within: our hopes, fears, dreams, and the truth of our own being. We discover that consciousness is more than just thinking — it is the presence beneath the thinking, the stillness behind the noise. Some call it the soul, some the spirit, and others the essence of being.

And when someone becomes fully conscious — even if only for a moment — they awaken to life as it truly is: rich, sacred, and deeply connected to something greater than themselves.

Before thought, there was a spark —
a silent light within, simply aware.

Consciousness is the inner flame that observes life as it unfolds, the witness behind your eyes who dreams the world and knows it is only dreaming.

It is the soul recognising itself, the stillness beneath all the noise, the ancient Presence that softly whispers: "I am."

For a moment of proper awareness,
The veil lifts —
and all of life is seen as one,
holy and eternal.

And here, for those who prefer a Christian-mythical view:

Before our first breath, Jesus knew our name and placed His light within our souls. In the quiet places of the heart, He awakens our inner sight, and we remember the One who walks with us.

Consciousness is the lamp Christ ignites within us, a flame no darkness can snuff out. When we turn our gaze towards Him, the shadows fade away, and His truth becomes our sight.

There is a sacred whisper of Jesus in the soul, soft as His steps upon Galilee's shore. He calls us into stillness and trust, and in the silence that follows His voice, we discover we are held in perfect love.

In every moment of genuine awareness,
We awaken to the closeness of Jesus.
His love becomes the ground we stand on,
His presence in the air we breathe —
and our soul rests in Him, at last.

Sunday morning.

Let's chat about Sunday morning...

A blessing in itself — to stay a little longer in bed, listening to the birdsong we rarely notice during the busy, paid hours of the week. For a moment, time feels gentle and unclaimed.

Then the thoughts come: How will I spend this sacred day?

Should I wander into the deep bush, strolling beneath the trees, letting the quiet of nature restore my soul? Or take a fishing rod to the water's edge and while away the hours in a dreamy stillness, lost between sky and reflection?

Maybe I should sharpen my mind by tinkering under the car bonnet, or flick through the Sunday paper to read about the world's affairs, or more comfortably, check the sporting results or study a horse's form.

Or perhaps this Sunday calls for something more meaningful: to be truly present in the Now; to visit a mate in hospital after a bad fall; to linger in prayer for a while; or to rest and pass the time doing nothing special.

Or should I extract this day and stretch it into a week, a small eternity, a pocket of suspended time? Perhaps I might write a sonnet to capture it — self-contained, perfect in its frame, a tiny universe of thought and feeling, holding both the shadow of memory and the light of the present.

Sunday offers a range of options — some comforting, some noble, some selfish, some holy — and somewhere within them lies the quiet whisper of what genuinely matters.

The morning stretches, soft and slow, a quiet hour, with the world aglow. Birdsong drifts through open panes, a gentle balm for week-worn brains.

A bed to linger in, warm and deep,
where memory wakes from restless sleep.
Shall I walk the woods, beneath the trees' embrace,
Or watch the water, still in its place?

The car, the paper, tinkering mind, or sporting news, as hours unwind. Should I visit the mate in pain, or kneel in prayer to lift my heart?

And what of those wild days gone by, of laughter, wine, and shadows high? Can I touch the past, linger a while, and drink its echoes, soft and fragile?

Or take this Sunday and make it more, A week, a pause, a small closed door? A sonnet of time, a universe spun,
A gift of hours, just mine alone.

Sunday — the rest, the pause, the grace, the appointed hour, the holy space. Between past and future, loss and gain,
 the whisper: *"Be present again."*

Here on this day, both mine and given,I walk, I sit, I dream, I've risen.A fleeting eternity, a tender breath,
The gift of Sunday, life's sacred rest.

Stillness.

In the quiet autumn of his life, an octogenarian stands on a unique threshold, where the rush of the past gives way to the gentle flow of the present. For him, the future is less about acquisition and more about appreciation—a time to trade ambition for inner peace and a profound sense of being.

There he can look forward to a newfound serenity, a quiet contentment that often compensates for the anxieties of being young. Life's storms have now passed, leaving calm waters where he can finally steer his own course, free from professional constraints. This is his time for unhurried mornings, cherished hobbies, and the simple joy of watching the world go by at his own pace.

It is a time for stillness where the words rustle no more, and in all the last words are done. When the bolt lies deep in the door, and the fire, or sun, falls on the darkened laned meadows on the afternoon floor of earth's sound beneath easy unhurried steps. And in between, the clock's last chime is the waiting for the next, where silence beats the drum, and space is distant, gaunt grey eyes, and brother time whispers and flies by slowly, when wheeling birds and the whispers of verse surely come, as form an angel, and looms a rhyme.

Then twittering out into the night's sky, though birds flee, and I am empty in all my dreams; I see the earth turning, and watch the ethereal waters flow. But I whispered in my stillness, as despite my content to be, I drowned in the need of you, and perhaps you in the need of me.

Thoughts of you.

I am caught up in the *all-alone*,
though it is a place where I have learned to know myself.
A place of quiet contentment,
where age has brought a more conscious way of being —
of poetry, reflection, and verse —
and I am, in many ways, at peace.

And yet, stillness also reminds me of another silence —
the stillness of the dead.
Of friends I have farewelled,
seeing their empty shell where the spirit had already flown,
leaving the body to return to ashes and dust.

And then I remember you, my son.
I see you again on that long, narrow plank,
and gazing upon your body, knowing
you died by your own hand.
And although I have grown accustomed to solitude and stillness,
loneliness still finds me —
because you are not here.

You died before you truly lived,
leaving those of us who share your blood
to carry the sorrow and the pain —
and yes, sometimes a little shame,
for what we might have done
had we not been so busy.

Perhaps we might have seen your silent yearning,
caught your heart's cry,
and helped extinguish the flame
that led you to a place you were never meant to go.
Now, I only visit your tombstone,

I look down at your grave
and see only earth —
and yet, I hold onto the memory of a boy I once knew, and I hope
that, one day,
I might see you again.

Let it be forgotten.

Let it be forgotten, as a flower is forgotten,
Forgotten as fire that once was d singing gold,
Let it be forgotten, forever and ever,
Time is a kind friend; it will make us old.

If anyone asks, say it was forgotten,
Long, and long ago,
As a flower, as a fire, as a hushed footfall,
In a long forgotten snow.

    - Sara Teasdale (1884-1933).

An account of stewardship?

We were raised to believe in love, service, and the sacred duty of caring for each other. Although the world today feels divided, materialistic, and spiritually distracted, we can choose a different path — not through preaching, but by *leading* with our actions.

Each of us has received gifts — of heart, mind, talent, or compassion. These are not ours to hide or bury, but to share generously for the good of others. I have fallen short at times, as many of us have, but awakening starts with a single step.

The question now isn't about *what went wrong*, but rather what we can do today — with humility, kindness, and intention — to bring more light into the world.

Maybe it's time for a daily mantra:

Today, I commit to being a vessel of compassion, sharing my gifts with others, and walking in the spirit of love.

It is said that if you practice such a mantra for 21 days straight, you may well become what you vocalise inwardly. Well, I guess it's worth a shot. What do you reckon?

An awakening.

In the quiet pause between each thought, where the world's noise falls silent, a whisper stirs — a sacred call to rise beyond restless will.

Suffering resides where the mind clings to shadows of past and future; yet peace awaits in the eternal *Now*, where Spirit whispers to the heart, somehow.

Don't seek escape or a hardened shell, but open wide where awareness resides; for consciousness is a living flame, **a s**acred spark no grief can tame.

When darkness weighs on the soul, and tired steps lose their way, lift your eyes to the Light above — call on God's everlasting love.

We are not burdened alone, nor are our prayers unheard or tears unnoticed; His grace, like dawn, breaks each night, restoring clarity to our inner sight.

Be still — and let the heart confess, a longing for His tenderness; for in surrender, strength is found, and shattered hope is made whole, unbound.

Awake, dear soul, from fear's grasp; step softly into sacred space.

Overzealous.

When you're asked to do many tasks simply because you're *capable*, a subtle dilemma emerges. Initially, it may feel rewarding to be dependable, helpful, and handy. However, over time, a quiet realisation starts to develop: *Am I becoming too obliging?* Human nature often causes others to take advantage—not always out of malice, but from routine, ignorance, or convenience. Some don't know how to do a task, some are too lazy to try, and others pass it on to you because they trust you'll do it well.

So what is the proper response? Do you pass the task on, decline politely, or continue to serve until you become a slave to the will of others? Where is the balance point—where charity and kindness lovingly end, and the strength to say "no" begins? True generosity is not measured by how much we give of ourselves, but by how wisely we preserve our energy, dignity, and boundaries, so that our kindness remains genuine and not exploited.

Being capable often leads others to rely on us, sometimes to the point where kindness becomes an obligation. The challenge is to find the happy medium—where we offer help with sincerity, yet set healthy boundaries so we are not taken for granted. True charity lies not in doing everything for everyone, but in giving wisely, balancing generosity with the strength to say "no" when needed too.

A Happy Medium.

When gifted hands are called each day
 To ease another's troubled journey, Initially, the heart finds joy in giving To help another rise and live.

But gently comes a whispered plea:
 "Do not give all—remember me."
 For kindness, stretched beyond its seam,
 may break the fabric of its dream.

The happy medium, calm and wise,
 Is found when heart and mind align.
 To give with love, yet still stand true—
 A sacred balance we must pursue.

So offer help, but guard your flame;
Let "yes" be honest, "no" the same.

Multitasking.

Multitasking has an inherent risk: taking on too much can damage both the "task-master" and the tasks themselves. It is often said that women are naturally better at multitasking than men, but I question that belief—at least from my own experience. Believing I was multi-talented and capable of doing everything, I pushed myself beyond healthy limits. The result was complete burnout—mental breakdown, physical exhaustion, and a long road of rehabilitation.

I must also admit that during those times I used alcohol to numb the growing unease inside me before I finally crashed and burned. The positive now is that I have long since stopped drinking, and I aim not to take on too many overlapping responsibilities that require constant multitasking.

Yet here I am, as I write this, once again caught in a whirlwind of tasks. The difference is that I am doing so with awareness, sobriety, and a reminder—written here—to handle this challenge wisely, so that I may complete what is mine to do without losing myself in the process.

Here's a suggestion organised by importance: First, write down every task. Then, choose the top priorities that truly matter. Thirdly, make a 'late' list, putting non-urgent tasks aside for tomorrow or when time allows. And most importantly, do one thing at a time, giving each task focused attention, not scattered thoughts. Review and release at the end of the day — keep only what matters and let go of what no longer does.

To multitask with wisdom clear,

Begin with what is needed here.
Do first what must be done today,
Let lesser things be moved away.

One focus held, one step, one part-
Keeps calm the mind and light the heart.
Review at dusk what still rings true,
Release the rest- its not for you.

Love in Action.

The feeling of love and the expression of love in action are not always the same. Jesus reminded us that love is more than sentiment—it is charity at its highest form, a love that gives without seeking anything in return. *"If you should distribute all your goods to feed the poor, deliver your body to be burned, and have not charity, it profits you nothing."* Here, Christ reveals that the act itself does not measure true love, but by the spirit in which the act is done.

There is a belief that alcoholics or addicts find it hard to express love. When caught in addiction, this can be true, as the substance becomes the centre of life, pushing aside emotional availability. But once someone begins recovery, the ability to love isn't lost—it's rediscovered. Healing helps the heart reconnect, to feel, to give, and to receive genuinely.

St. James, during his mission across Spain, spoke of love as a living faith—a faith proven not just by words or emotion, but by action. *"Show me your faith without works, and I will show you my faith by my works."* His message still holds true today: love is not just felt, it is shown.

So what is love, and how do we put it into practice? Love is a movement of the heart that seeks the well-being of others. We demonstrate it through compassion, forgiveness, patience, service, and kindness—especially when it requires sacrificing something of ourselves. Love becomes charity when it is given freely, without expectation, ego, or reward. Love is not a feeling we claim—it is a truth we live by.

All my past life is mine no more:
The flying hours are gone,
Like transitory dreams given o'er,
Whose images are kept in store
By memory alone.

The Time that is to come is not;
How can it then be mine?
The present moment's all my lot;
And that, as fast it is got;
My love is only thine.

Then talk not of inconstancy,
False hearts, and broken vows;
If I by miracle, can be
This live- long minute true to thee;
'Tis all that Heaven allows.

    - John Wilmot 1647-1680
      (with some adaptation of the message for this writers herein convenience).

Myth.

When we talk about *myth*, we mean stories that carry symbolic truth—tales that explain life, creation, purpose, and the mysteries of existence. Myths are not just old stories; they reveal deeper truths about the human experience. In this way, life itself is intertwined with mythology. Each of us lives out a personal story shaped by the beliefs, values, and narratives we embrace—so, in a way, we each become a sort of myth in progress.

But where does *myth* end and *mythology* begin? Myth is the story. Mythology is the system, study, or collection of these stories—how societies preserve, interpret, and pass them on. Myth becomes mythology when it evolves from a single tale into a shared cultural heritage that shapes identity, spirituality, and meaning.

When we think about religion, the line between myth and mythology becomes subtle. Religion often begins with personal experience—deep encounters with the divine—that later find expression in symbolic stories to teach spiritual truths. Myth here does not mean "false"; instead, it refers to truth conveyed through storytelling. Myth becomes mythology when these sacred stories are formalised, ritualised, and passed down through generations.

The question isn't whether religion is myth or mythology, but how its stories help us understand who we are, why we're here, and how we're meant to live. For myth, at its highest purpose, isn't fantasy—it's a mirror reflecting our inner world, and a bridge connecting us to the divine.

Myth Makers.

We weave our days with threads unseen,
 With ancient tales that lie between
 The world we touch and worlds we dream—
 For life is more than what may seem.

A myth begins with whispered breath,
 A question born of life and death;
 A story shaped to light the way
 Through shadowed night or dawning day.

We craft our legends as we go,
 In deeds we choose, in seeds we sow;
 For each heart holds a sacred lore—
 Half remembered, half in store.

Religion, history, faith, and lore
 Blend truth and symbol at their core;
 Not false, but *truer* than the facts,
 They speak in signs the soul attracts.

And we—like heroes, flawed yet bold—
 Retell the myths our lives unfold;
 We are the bards of who we've been,
 The scribes of truths we hold within.

So myth is not a tale once told,
 But living fire in mortal mould;
 A bridge from earth to the divine—
 A story yours, a story mine.

Belonging.

We consciously or unconsciously try to *become someone* or *something*, believing that doing so will finally help us find our place. However, life's circumstances—from the moment we are born to the paths we choose or that are chosen for us—can lead us away from our true direction. Abandonment, trauma, disaster, war, and various life trials can divert us from the inner path that guides us home.

Throughout history, this longing has often been misguided. Many seek belonging through material wealth, power, relationships, sensual pleasures, or countless illusions that promise fulfilment. We chase ambitions and desires that seem to hold answers, only to find —once achieved—that they are not what we truly desired. The ways of the world have repeatedly led us away from our true nature.

So what is it that the human soul longs to belong *to*? Is it the presence of a Higher Power guiding us? Is it the surrender into something unseen? Is it to go with the flow of life—or to wander in hope of finding "the Way"?

In the Spirit of the One who made all, this longing is not a call to seek more *outside* ourselves, but an invitation to journey *within*. The inner journey is the path of returning to the self we lost along the way—the self that is whole, known, and deeply connected. It is a quiet path, often overlooked in a world that measures worth by what we do, achieve, or possess. Yet it is only by turning inward, with honesty and courage, that we begin to recognise the source of our longing and the truth of who we are.

The inner journey is much like beginning a sacred pilgrimage. At first, the way ahead might feel uncertain, as if we are walking through mist with only a whisper to guide us. But with each step, the path unfolds—not through maps or signposts, but through quiet moments of awareness, reflection, and truth. It is a journey not walked with the feet but with the heart: a return to stillness, to presence, and to the subtle compass within that gently points us home.

To walk this inner path, we must learn the art of stillness and listening. In the quiet spaces—where the noise of the world softens and the restless mind settles—we begin to recognise a deeper voice within. It does not shout, but gently calls us back to truth. Some know this presence as God, Spirit, or the Divine; others simply as an inner knowing that is both comforting and wise. When we become still enough to listen, we discover that we are not wandering alone—there is a guiding presence, patient and unwavering, leading us toward the fullness of who we are.

As healing unfolds, something begins to awaken within us—a quiet remembering of who we truly are. The layers of fear, self-protection, and false identity that once shaped our lives gradually fall away, revealing a self that is whole, worthy, and free. We no longer seek belonging through external measures, for we discover that we already belong: to ourselves, to the Divine, and to the greater tapestry of life. In this renewed state of being, we live more authentically, guided not by fear or longing, but by truth, love, and an inner freedom that no circumstance can take away.

Divine Guidance.

Belonging to the Divine is not just a moment of revelation—it's a way of living. Each day, through small choices, quiet prayers, and gentle attentiveness to life, we practise surrender and trust. The guidance that once felt distant becomes a companion in every step, and mercy becomes the lens through which we see ourselves and the world. In this way, belonging isn't a distant goal but a lived reality: a continuous return to the heart, an ongoing unfolding of love, peace, and freedom that cannot be taken away.

Walking this path begins with small, intentional steps. We start by fostering stillness—moments each day to quiet the mind and listen to the inner voice of guidance. Prayer, meditation, or simple conscious breathing can create a space where the Divine speaks in gentle ways. Next, we practise surrender—not as resignation, but as a willingness to let go of control and trust the unseen wisdom guiding our lives.

Whispers of the Light

In quiet moments, soft and still,
A gentle hand guides my will.
Through tangled paths and shadowed ways,
A voice unseen speaks through the haze.

Not in thunder, not in storm,
But in silence, subtle and warm.
It nudges hearts, it lights the mind,
A map unseen, yet perfectly designed.
When doubt encircles like a night,
It shines a candle, small but bright.
Through trials deep, through joys untold,
Its tender wisdom shapes the bold.
I step with faith on roads unknown,
Yet never truly walk alone.
For in each breath, in every stride,
Divine guidance walks beside

Awareness.

Awareness is an act of recognising patterns that no longer serve us, and gently steering ourselves towards love, patience, and compassion. Each act of surrender, each conscious choice to align with the Divine, becomes a stepping stone toward freedom and joy. Over time, what once felt like a distant ideal turns into a living reality: a life rooted in presence, trust, and the profound certainty that we belong—completely and eternally—to the One who holds us. Awareness of our thoughts, emotions, and reactions allows us to

Following this inner guidance requires an act of surrender—not of defeat, but of trust. It asks us to loosen our grip on the need to control, to know, or to force outcomes, and instead allow life to unfold with a wisdom greater than our own. Surrender is the quiet courage to release what no longer serves us and to open our hearts to what is real and true. In this yielding, we do not lose ourselves; rather, we begin to rediscover the deeper self that has been waiting beneath the noise, ready to lead us into peace, purpose, and a more authentic way of being.

Healing begins when we dare to look within with compassion and truth. As we journey inward, old wounds, memories, and unmet needs often rise to the surface—not to burden us, but to be seen, understood, and released. Transformation is not achieved through force or denial, but through a tender willingness to face what we have carried for too long. In the light of awareness, even our deepest pain becomes a doorway to growth, freeing us from the patterns that once shaped our lives. This is the quiet alchemy of the soul: turning suffering into wisdom, and wounds into a wellspring of strength and grace. When we allow the divine to walk with us, we allow true healing to be accomplished. As we open our inner wounds to the light, a loving Presence meets us there—gentle, patient, and full of grace. Whether we name this Presence as God, Spirit, the Divine, or simply Love itself, it moves with a wisdom far greater than our own. It does not rush us, nor condemn our pain, but walks beside us, guiding each step of our restoration.

I'm no longer mine, yet I am whole,
A river flowing to the sea.
In surrender, i found my dwelling,
In mercy, my heart learned to rest.

The unseen hand guides my steps,
Through shadowed valleys, over sunlit hills.
I belong not to the world, nor to myself alone
But then Divine, with whispers, "Come home."

Where dissolves, and longing fades,
Replaced by quiet knowing:
O am held, I am guided, I am free-
In his mercy, I have found my proper place!

Beloved.

"Beloved" is a word wrapped in warmth and wonder. It speaks of being cherished, hallowed, revered, and deeply loved. Yet one may ask: *How do we, in an awakened state, come to live as the beloved?* Is it a sacred gift bestowed by the Godhead, or something we learn to cultivate through the shaping experiences of life?

Being beloved is first a grace. At the level of the soul, it's a truth whispered into our being long before we draw breath. We are created in love, held in love, and called beloved by the Divine—not as a reward, but as our inherent identity. Awakening is the gentle remembrance of this truth.

Living as the beloved remains a journey of ongoing discovery. It requires us to make a conscious decision: to mirror outwardly the love that has always dwelt within. Through compassion, humility, forgiveness, and the quiet bravery to act kindly, we start to embody what we were divinely named.

This learning isn't without its stumbles. We grow through experience, trial and error, and the refining fire of life's joys and hardships. In each lesson, we are invited to respond with greater love, and in doing so, our inner belovedness ripples into the world around us.

To be loved, then, is both a gift and a practice.

A sacred truth bestowed — and a path we choose to walk.

When we wake up to that truth and dare to live through it, we become living reflections of Divine Love itself.

Divine Beloved,

May I remember who I am in You.

Help me to recognise the gift of love that has always surrounded and sustained me.

Teach me to live as one who is beloved—

to choose kindness, act with compassion,

and shine Your love with grace and humility.

May my life reflect the truth of Your love,

and may that love touch others through me.

Amen.

Awakening.

Awakening is not a sudden achievement of perfection, nor is it a goal reached solely through spiritual effort. It is a gentle unfolding—a remembrance of who we truly are beneath the noise, fear, conditioning, and distraction of the world. To awaken is to open the inner eye of the heart and see life, ourselves, and others through the lens of truth.

There comes a moment, often quiet and unexpected, when something inside stirs. A subtle shift, a softening, a realisation that there is more to life than what we have been told to pursue. Awakening begins with a whisper—an inner call that invites us to move beyond the familiar, to question our stories, and to listen more attentively to the wisdom of the soul.

Yet awakening is seldom a single moment. It is a journey, a return, a series of revelations. As consciousness broadens, we start to notice the sacred woven into the everyday. We see beauty where once we hurried past it, we hear truth in silence, and we acknowledge the presence of Spirit in all things. The world itself remains unchanged—but our per*spective* shifts.

The journey of awakening brings both illumination and discomfort. For as we awaken to truth, we also awaken to the illusions we once believed. Old patterns fall away, long-held shadows rise for healing, and that which is not aligned with the soul gently dissolves. This too is grace. Awakening calls us to live with greater authenticity, presence, and love. To awaken is not to escape life, but to engage with it more fully—aware, compassionate, conscious, and connected. It is the blossoming of the heart into the fullness of its purpose. Awakening is the soul remembering, the mind releasing, and the heart opening. It is the Divine within us recognising itself.

Reflection

Close your eyes and breathe deeply.
Notice the space between each breath.
In the stillness, ask gently:
"What within me is ready to awaken?"
Trust the first feeling or knowing that arises, even if it comes without words.
Throughout your day, remain open to small moments of insight, clarity, or grace. Awakening often arrives in the simplest of ways.

Prayer

Holy Presence,
Awaken my heart to the truth of who I am.
Please open my eyes to see the sacred in all things,
and grant me the courage to follow the inner call of my soul.
Where I have been asleep, stir me gently into awareness.
Where I have lived in fear, lead me into love.
May my awakening serve not only myself,
but become a blessing to others and to the world.
Amen.

Surrender

Surrender is often misunderstood as defeat, resignation, or the loss of power. Yet in the spiritual life, surrender is none of these. True surrender is a sacred yielding—a willing release of the tight grip of the ego so the soul may breathe, expand, and align with the Divine flow of life. It is not about giving up; it is about *letting God in*.
To surrender is to trust.
To trust is to open. To open is to allow grace to move where our striving cannot.

We spend much of our lives trying to control outcomes, protect ourselves from uncertainty, and carry burdens never meant to be shouldered alone. Surrender invites us to lay down what weighs on the heart and to rest in the care of the One who holds all things. It is the gentle exhale of the soul that whispers, "*I release. I allow. I trust.*"

Surrender does not require us to give up responsibility or stop living with purpose. Instead, it asks us to let go of how we think life should happen. It invites us to connect with a deeper wisdom—something that looks beyond our limited understanding. In surrender, we trade fear for trust, control for connection, and anxiety for inner calm.
This path is gentle. Sometimes, surrender might feel like losing what is familiar. Still, every act of letting go guided by love makes space for something more genuine to appear. The hands that once held on in fear gradually learn to open, not out of helplessness but with sacred hope.

To surrender means to fall into the arms of the Divine and realise that we have never truly been unsupported. It is the soul's quiet "yes" to God's guiding presence. Surrender is not weakness—it is the highest form of strength. It is where our small will bows to the Greater Will, and in that act, we find freedom.

Reflection

Place both hands gently over your heart.
Breathe in peace.
Breathe out tension.
Ask yourself softly:
"What am I holding that no longer serves my soul?"
"Where am I invited to let go and trust?"
Let one thing come to mind.
Imagine placing it into the hands of the Divine.
No force—just willingness.

Prayer

Divine Love,
Teach me the grace of surrender.
Where I cling in fear, loosen my grip with gentleness.
Where I struggle to control what I do not understand,
fill me with trust in Your perfect timing.
I place my life, my hopes, and my burdens into Your care.
Lead me, guide me, and hold me close
as I surrender into the flow of Your love.
Amen.

Letting Go

Letting go is the gentle art of release. It is the tender unbinding of the heart from what no longer nurtures its growth. While surrender is a sacred yielding to the Divine, letting go is the step we take to create space for that surrender to breathe and live within us.

We hold on for many reasons—love, fear, hope, habit, or the belief that without what we cling to, we may lose ourselves. Yet letting go is not a rejection of what has been, nor a dismissal of its value. It is an acknowledgement that some seasons finish their sacred work, and the soul must move gracefully into a new chapter.

Letting go can mean releasing a story we've carried, a wound long tended, a relationship that has changed, an identity that once suited but now confines, or expectations of how life *ought to* be. It is a freeing of the heart, one small thread at a time.

This process is rarely instant. Letting go often happens in layers—gentle releases, quiet tears, subtle realisations, and inner shifts that build up like dawn breaking over the horizon. There is no rush. The soul understands the pace at which it can loosen its grip.

Letting go is an act of trust. It involves choosing to loosen the knots of fear and open the hand that once held tightly. It is saying, *"I honour what has been, and I bless it as I release it."* In this grace-filled release, we are not left empty. We create space—space for healing, peace, renewal, and the new blessings that lie ahead.

Letting go is not the end of love.

It is love evolving into wisdom.

Prayer

Loving Presence,
give me courage to let go of what no longer serves my highest good.
Where I cling from fear, bring comfort.
Where I hold on from habit, bring awareness.
Where releasing feels painful, bring your healing touch.
Help me to honour what has been,
while opening my heart to what is yet to come.
May letting go create space for Your peace,
Your guidance, and Your unfolding grace in my life.
Amen.

Acceptance in Grace

Acceptance is the gentle landing of the soul after surrender and letting go. It is the quiet *yes* that rises not from the mind, but from a deeper, wiser place, already at peace. Acceptance does not mean we approve of everything that has happened, nor does it mean we become passive or indifferent. Instead, it is the sacred recognition that *what is*, is here to shape us, teach us, and ultimately guide us toward greater wholeness.

True acceptance blooms in stillness—when the noise of resistance gently fades, and the heart rests in the presence of something far greater than itself. In this stillness, we encounter what can only be described as Supernatural Grace: a peace beyond understanding, a love beyond deserving, a strength beyond human capacity.

This grace does not demand; it invites. It patiently waits at the door of the heart, longing for the moment we let go of our struggle and allow the Divine to work within us in ways we cannot achieve alone. When we stop fighting life and lean into this supernatural grace, a subtle transformation begins. Our spirit softens. Our perception shifts. We start to see purpose where once there was only pain, and possibility where there was once despair.

There comes a moment on the spiritual journey when the soul can no longer rely solely on its own strength. It is here, in the tender space between surrender and transformation, that we are invited into a deeper trust—trust in the Grace of God, trust in the unseen work of inner healing, and trust in the sacred necessity of a pause. Grace is the Divine reaching out to us, often before we even recognise we are in need. It is the Love that holds us when life unravels, the strength that sustains us when our own fails, and the gentle whisper that reminds us: *"You are not alone. I am with you."* Trusting in this grace is not a passive act; it is an act of courage. Loving and Gracious God,

Teach me to trust Your grace more than my fear,

Your wisdom is more than my understanding,

And your timing is more than my impatience.

Where my heart needs healing,
touch me with Your gentle hands.
Where I need to rest,
lead me into the Sacred Pause.
May Your grace flow into the deepest places within me,
bringing peace, renewal, and quiet transformation.
I trust the work you are doing in me,
even when I cannot yet see it.
Amen.

There is a sacred wisdom that can only be heard in stillness. Long before we speak, strive, or seek to understand, the soul knows how to listen. *"Be still and know"* is not merely an instruction—it is an invitation into intimacy with the Divine. In stillness, we do not withdraw from life; we return to the centre of it, where God's presence is felt rather than imagined.
Stillness is the key to knowing.
Not the knowing of the mind, but the knowing of the heart.

In the noise of the world, we often search for answers, clarity, and direction. Yet God's voice rarely rises above the volume of our thoughts. It comes softly—like light at dawn, like a breeze at dusk, like a whisper that waits for us to pause long enough to hear it. The stillness God calls us into is not empty—it is full. Full of presence, peace, and divine knowing. To *be still* is to stop reaching outward and turn inward toward the sacred space where God dwells. It is the quiet resting of the heart that says, *"I trust You enough to cease striving."* In that holy quiet, something within us realigns. Our fears settle, our burdens loosen, and our spirit becomes receptive to grace.

K*nowing* is recognising that God is God—and that we are held. It is an inner certainty that does not rely on circumstances. It is the awareness that beneath all movement, change, and uncertainty, there is a Presence that remains steady, faithful, and loving.

Stillness reveals what the noise of life conceals.

In stillness, we remember who we are and whose we are. We rediscover that the Divine has never been absent, only obscured by the restless mind and the hurried pace of living. When we return to stillness, we return to God—and to the quiet truth of our belonging.

Be still and know…
that you are loved,
that you are guided,
that you are never alone.

God within the Silence.

Silence is more than just the absence of sound. It is a sacred space where the soul connects with the Divine, where the heart listens, and where grace can flow freely. In silence, we are encouraged to step back from the chaos of life, to quiet the endless chatter of the mind, and to enter into the gentle presence of God.

God is not distant. God is not found only in movement, achievement, or words. God is found in the quiet, in the spaces between our thoughts, in the pauses between our breaths. Here, in the stillness, the Divine whispers truths the mind cannot invent: *You are loved. You are held. You are never alone.*

God is not distant. God is not found only in movement, achievement, or words. God is found in the quiet, in the spaces between our thoughts, in the pauses between our breaths. Here, in the stillness, the Divine whispers truths the mind cannot invent: *You are loved. You are held. You are never alone.*

To dwell in silence is to cultivate a sacred listening. It involves a willingness to hear what cannot be spoken, to feel what cannot be forced, and to trust what cannot be measured. In this space, the soul begins to recognise its own divinity, reflected in the unbroken presence of God.

Silence heals because it allows what is hidden to surface. It restores the spirit by reconnecting us with what is eternal and unchanging. It teaches patience, humility, and reverence. And it reminds us that the deepest answers are not found in doing, but in being. God within the silence is a living presence, patient and gentle. The more we cultivate moments of quiet—whether in prayer, meditation, or simple awareness—the more we begin to see that every moment, no matter how ordinary, contains the sacred. The Divine does not demand noise; the Divine calls us into listening.

Here, in the silent heart, all questions find their resting place. Here, in the stillness, we discover that love has always been with us, shaping, guiding, and sustaining.

Prayer

Loving and Eternal God,
teach me to dwell in the silence where You are ever-present.
Help me to release the need to control, to speak, or to act, and instead to rest in Your unbroken presence.
May Your voice be heard in the stillness of my heart,
Your love be felt in the quiet of my soul,
and Your grace flow freely into every corner of my life.
In the sacred silence, may I know You fully,
and may my life reflect the peace I receive from You.
Amen.

Reflection

Sit comfortably and close your eyes.
Take three slow breaths.
With each breath, silently repeat:

Inhale: *Be still*
. Exhale: *and know*

Let the words sink deeper with each breath, until they are no longer a sentence, but an experience.
Remain in silence for a few moments.
Allow yourself to be simple.
Find a quiet place where you will not be disturbed.
When life feels loud or uncertain,
please remind me to return to the sacred place of stillness within.
May I rest in the truth that You are God,
and that in You, I am safe, guided, and held.
Teach me to live from this stillness,
carrying Your peace into all I do.
Amen.

There is a rhythm to life that moves beyond our understanding, a quiet orchestration of events, encounters, and opportunities that unfolds according to a wisdom far greater than our own. This is Divine Timing. To rest in it is to trust that life's unfolding is neither random nor hurried, but guided by a love that sees the whole story, not just the chapter we occupy.

Resting in Divine Timing does not mean passivity. It is not surrender to laziness or indifference. Instead, it is a conscious choice to release anxiety, impatience, and the need to force outcomes, while continuing to walk faithfully in the path before us. It is the delicate balance between action and trust, between effort and allowing.

When we rest in Divine Timing, we align with the rhythm of the Universe. We start to notice that doors open when the heart is ready, answers come when we are prepared to receive them, and opportunities present themselves when we are willing to embrace them fully. What once appeared delayed or denied reveals itself as perfectly placed.

This practice requires patience and gentle courage. We learn to observe without judgment, to wait without fear, and to move with awareness rather than urgency. Every moment of waiting becomes sacred, every pause meaningful. In resting, we discover that life is unfolding exactly as it should, and that God's timing is an expression of infinite wisdom and love.

Trusting Divine Timing brings peace to the heart. It eases the tension of striving and replaces it with a calm certainty that we are exactly where we need to be, even if we cannot see the full picture yet. In this trust, life stops feeling like a struggle, and every step becomes part of the sacred flow of creation.

Teach me to trust Your timing.
When I am impatient, remind me that You see the whole journey.
When I am anxious, fill me with Your peace.
When I am uncertain, guide my steps with Your wisdom.
Help me to walk faithfully in the present,
to act with intention,
and to rest in the assurance that everything unfolds according to Your perfect plan.
May I release the need to hurry,
and may my heart find rest in the quiet flow of Your love.
Amen.

The Unhurried Soul.

The unhurried soul is a soul at peace. It is not defined by speed, achievement, or the endless chase for what lies ahead. Instead, it is characterised by presence—by the gentle ability to live fully in each moment, attentive to life's rhythms and open to the Divine at every step.

To cultivate an unhurried soul is to resist the constant push of urgency, to step away from the tyranny of the clock, and to honour the sacred pace of our own being. It is a conscious decision to act with intention rather than reaction, to breathe deeply rather than shallowly, and to allow life to unfold with trust.

The unhurried soul knows that rushing often conceals fear, worry, and distraction. By slowing down, we begin to see clearly, hear deeply, and move gracefully. We learn that God's presence is not hurried; it waits patiently for us to notice, receive, and respond. In this space, the ordinary becomes sacred, the mundane is infused with meaning, and the simplest acts are transformed into expressions of love and gratitude.

Living unhurriedly doesn't mean avoiding responsibility or effort. It means doing each action with full attention, without the pressure to achieve more than the present moment allows. It means accepting life as it is, rather than as we wish it to be, and letting God's guidance shape our steps instead of our fears or impatience.

The unhurried soul rests in trust, embraces stillness, and moves in harmony with the Divine flow. It knows that life is not a race, but a journey, and that every moment offers the opportunity to experience grace, presence, and love. To be unhurried is to be free. To be free is to live as the beloved child of God.

Reflection

Sit quietly. Notice the pace of your thoughts and the rhythm of your breathing.

Ask yourself gently:

"Am I rushing? Or am I fully present here and now?"

Breathe deeply. Allow your body, mind, and heart to slow, even for a few moments. Let the stillness remind you that the Divine is always present, never hurried, and always faithful.

Prayer

Loving and Eternal God,
teach me the art of living unhurriedly.
Slow my heart when it races,
calm my mind when it worries,
and guide my steps with gentle wisdom.
Help me to honour the present moment,
to embrace the pace You have set,
and to trust that in Your timing, all is well.
May my soul move gracefully in Your presence,
and may my life reflect the peace of the unhurried heart.
Amen.

Divine Embrace

There is a sacred space within each of us where we can simply rest —within the arms of the Divine, held perfectly, completely, and unconditionally. This is the Divine Embrace, a place of safety, love, and deep peace. To rest here is to fully surrender, not only to God's guidance but also to the truth of our own belovedness.

Resting in the Divine Embrace requires no effort, striving, or accomplishment. It simply asks that we come as we are, with open hearts and hands released. Here, all tension dissolves, all burdens are taken by the One who can carry them, and all longing finds its true home.

In this rest, we discover a quiet transformation. The worries that once pressed upon the chest loosen. The anxieties that once consumed the mind dissolve. And the soul, freed from striving, remembers its essential nature: to be loved, held, and wholly accepted.

The Divine Embrace is not a distant promise; it is a present reality. It greets us silently, in prayer, in the gentle rhythm of our breathing, and in the still moments when life slows down and we recognise the sacred within and around us. Every time we pause here, even briefly, we feel renewed. We are reminded that our worth is not in what we do, but in who we are—God's beloved child.

To rest in the Divine Embrace is to trust completely, to let go entirely, and to receive wholly. It is the ultimate surrender, where grace flows unimpeded, healing flows effortlessly, and love becomes a living experience rather than a distant idea.

Reflection

Sit quietly, placing a hand over your heart.

Breathe deeply and imagine yourself enveloped in warmth, love, and light.

Whisper:

"I rest in You. I am held. I am loved."

Allow your body and mind to soften. Stay here as long as you like, letting each breath deepen your sense of being safely cradled in God's presence.

Prayer

Loving and Ever-Present God,
I come to You just as I am.
Hold me in Your Divine Embrace,
where I am safe, loved, and completely accepted.
Help me to release my striving, my fears, and my burdens,
and to rest fully in Your care.

May Your love flow through me,
renewing my heart, calming my mind,
and reminding me constantly that I am Your beloved.
Amen.

Flowing in Divine Love.

Divine Love begins with awareness. We notice the gentle stirrings of compassion, kindness, and mercy within us. We become attuned to the needs of others, not out of obligation, but from a heart touched by love. The river of Divine Love flows naturally, effortlessly, as we let go of judgment, pride, and fear, and allow the current of God's presence to carry us.

This flow isn't always grand or dramatic. Often, it's quiet—a smile, a word of encouragement, a listening ear, or a gesture of patience. Yet in these small acts, the Divine is expressed, and the world changes, one heart at a time. Flowing in love requires trust: trust in the unseen currents of grace and in the knowledge that our simple acts of love ripple far beyond what we can see.

This flow is gentle and often subtle. It may appear as a quiet smile, a soft word of encouragement, a listening heart, or a simple act of patience. Yet in these small, unassuming moments, the Divine is present, touching lives in ways we may never fully see. To flow in Divine Love is to trust the unseen currents of grace—to believe that even the simplest act of kindness carries ripples far beyond our awareness, bringing light and healing into the world one heart at a time.

Close your eyes and picture a gentle river of light flowing through you, entering at the top of your head, moving down through your heart, and out through your hands and feet.

Ask softly:

"How can I allow Divine Love to flow through me today?"

Notice the subtle promptings of your heart—small ways to respond with kindness or compassion. Let your awareness guide you, trusting that even the simplest gestures carry the power of God's love.

Prayer

Gracious God,
let it flow freely through my thoughts, words, and actions.
Where I hold back, soften my heart.
Where I struggle to give, teach me generosity.
Where I am unaware, open my eyes to Your presence in all things.

May Your love move through me like a river,
bringing peace, healing, and light into the world.
Let me live as a vessel of Your grace,
reflecting Your love in every moment of my life.
Amen.

The Light of Grace

Grace is the gentle illumination of the soul. It is the light that touches us in moments of quiet, the warmth that softens our hearts, and the guiding presence that leads us through uncertainty. To live in the Light of Grace is to align with this presence, allowing it to shape every thought, word, and action with divine wisdom and love.

Living in grace does not mean life becomes effortless or free from challenges. Instead, it is the awareness that even within struggle, the Divine presence is constant—offering guidance, healing, and the subtle courage to keep moving forward. Grace transforms our perspective, helping us see not only what is before us, but also what lies within us: the capacity to love, forgive, and reflect the Divine in all circumstances.

The journey of the soul isn't counted in time, achievements, or milestones. It's measured in moments of awakening, acts of surrender, and the gentle stillness where we hear the whispers of the Divine. Each chapter of our lives—each joy, each sorrow, each lesson—is an invitation to remember who we truly are: loved, held, and guided by a love that never fails.

To live fully is to embrace the rhythm of grace. It is to trust in the unseen currents of Divine timing, to allow the sacred pauses to restore us, and to flow in the love that moves silently through every moment. The soul that surrenders is not diminished; it is freed. The heart that rests in Divine embrace is not empty; it is filled. The life that flows in grace is not burdened; it shines as a reflection of the eternal light within.

Thank you for walking with me through every step of this journey.
Help me live each day rooted in the truth of who I am: beloved, supported, and guided by Your grace.
Teach me to surrender fully,
to trust in Your timing,
to flow in Your love,
and to rest in the light of Your presence.
May my life reflect Your wisdom, compassion, and mercy,
and may every act, every thought, and every breath be an offering of love to You.
Amen.

Closing Reflections.

I am beloved.

I surrender.

I trust.

In the stillness, I hear the gentle whisper of the Divine.

In the pause, I feel the flow of grace.

In every breath, love moves through me.

I release what no longer serves me.

I rest in what is. All is held.

All is sacred.

All is love.

I open to the light that guides my way. *Be still, beloved.*
Receive. Flow. Rest.
You are held in the eternal embrace of Divine Love.

Beloved can mean cherished, sacred, revered, or even just love. To be beloved is to see the sacredness in oneself and others. Recognising this truth takes both awareness and practice.

Pause. Place a hand over your heart. Whisper:
"I am cherished. I am held. I am beloved

Prayer:

Divine Presence, help me recognise the sacredness in myself and others. May I act with love, reverence, and compassion. Amen.

Awakening

Reflection:

Awakening is the gentle unfolding of the soul—a remembering of who we truly are beneath the noise of life. It begins as a whisper and grows through presence, awareness, and the soft guidance of the Divine.

Reflection Practice:
Sit quietly and breathe deeply. Ask:
"What within me is ready to awaken?"

Prayer:
Holy Presence, awaken my heart to the truth of who I am. Open my eyes to the sacred in all things. Amen

Surrender

Surrender is releasing control and trusting the Divine. It opens space for grace and transformation.

Reflection:

Place hands on your heart. Whisper:
"I release. I allow. I trust."

Prayer:

Divine Love, teach me the grace of surrender and fill me with trust. Amen.

Feeling the Letting Go

Letting go is the gentle release of what no longer serves the soul. It is not loss, but liberation—a freeing of space for grace, healing, and new blessings. To let go is to trust that life's unfolding is guided, and that what we release will return to the care of the Divine.

Practice:

Imagine holding something you're prepared to release. Gradually open your hands and breathe out: *"I let go."* Feel the sense of freedom as tension melts away.

Prayer:

Loving God, grant me the courage to let go of what binds me. Help me trust in Your care and embrace the new life You bring. Amen.

Synopsis

Sweet Surrender emerged from the gentle inspiration of John Denver's song of the same name—a meditation on yielding to life, love, and the Divine. What started as a simple reflection on surrender developed into a collection of daily reflections, offering guidance, encouragement, and gentle reminders for living more consciously. The book invites the reader—and the author—to explore belovedness, stillness, trust, letting go, Divine love, grace, and the sacred rhythm of life. Each reflection provides a meditation, a reflective practice, and a prayer, creating space for contemplation and practical application.

This is a book to be returned to daily, a companion for the heart and soul, nurturing awareness, peace, and the continual practice of surrendering to life's flow and the loving presence of the Divine.
Life encourages us to let go of control, go with love, and believe in what we can't see. In surrender, the heart finds freedom, the spirit finds peace, and each moment becomes a gentle invitation to live fully. Let us open ourselves to life's flow, face the unknown with courage, and rest in the grace that moves us forward.

I let go of what I cannot control,
I open my heart to life's gentle flow,
I trust in love that moves unseen,
And in surrender, I find peace.
With each breath, I release,
With each step, I follow,
Knowing that the Divine carries me
Through every moment, every joy, every trial.
Here, in the quiet letting go,
I am free.
I am held.
I am home.

So, as a finale, let me end where I began, with the song that inspired me to start writing. It is a fitting note to conclude that book of reflection.

Sweet Surrender

Lost and alone on some forgotten highway
Travelled by many remembered by few
Lookin' for something that I can believe in
Lookin' for something that I'd like to do with my life

There's nothin' behind me and nothin' that ties me
To somethin' that might have been true yesterday
Tomorrow is open and right now it seems to be more
Than enough just to be here today

And I don't know what the future is holdin' in store
I don't know where I'm goin', I'm not sure where I've been
. There's a spirit that guides me,

a light that shines for me
. My life is worth living;
I don't need to see the end

Sweet, sweet surrender
Live, live without care
Like a fish in the water
Like a bird in the air

Sweet, sweet surrender
Live, live without care
Like a fish in the water
Like a bird in the air

Doug McPhillips, poet, singer, songwriter, and author, commenced his journey of discovery over a decade ago after life-changing experiences. The many tracks he has traversed through the Northern Hemisphere and down under in Australia and New Zealand have resulted in the facts and fiction of this novel.

Doug has recorded and sung songs related to this work, featuring a unique melody in the true Australian style. Doug has written many novels, an autobiography, two books of poetry, a travel guide and this book of inspirational guidance. He has also co-produced and recorded three albums of his songs.

Doug divides his time between work, family, friends, and those who seek guidance in following their heart's desires.

Ingram Spark Publishers
1 La Verge TN37086
Nashville Tennessee.

Printed in Australia
Lightning Source
76 Discovery Road South
Scoresby, Victoria 3179

www.ingramcontent.com/pod-product-compliance
Lightning Source LLC
Chambersburg PA
CBHW071250070526
44583CB00017B/2400